WORSHIP HITS FOR
UKULELE

ISBN 978-1-4803-6392-2

HAL•LEONARD®
CORPORATION

7777 W. BLUEMOUND RD. P.O. BOX 13819 MILWAUKEE, WI 53213

Visit Hal Leonard Online at
www.halleonard.com

CONTENTS

Above All

Words and Music by Paul Baloche and Lenny LeBlanc

won - ders the world __ has ev - er known; __ a - bove all

wealth and treas - ures of __ the earth, _____

there's no way __ to meas - ure what __ You're worth.

𝄋 Chorus

Cru - ci - fied, __ laid be - hind __ a stone, __ You

lived to die __ re - ject - ed and __ a - lone. __ Like a rose __

__ tram - pled on __ the ground, _____ You took __ the fall __

and thought of me ___ a - bove ___ all.

A - bove all

all.

all. Like a rose ___

Outro

tram - pled on ___ the ground, _____ You took ___ the fall ___

and thought of me ___ a - bove ___

all.

Forever Reign

Words and Music by Reuben Morgan and Jason Ingram

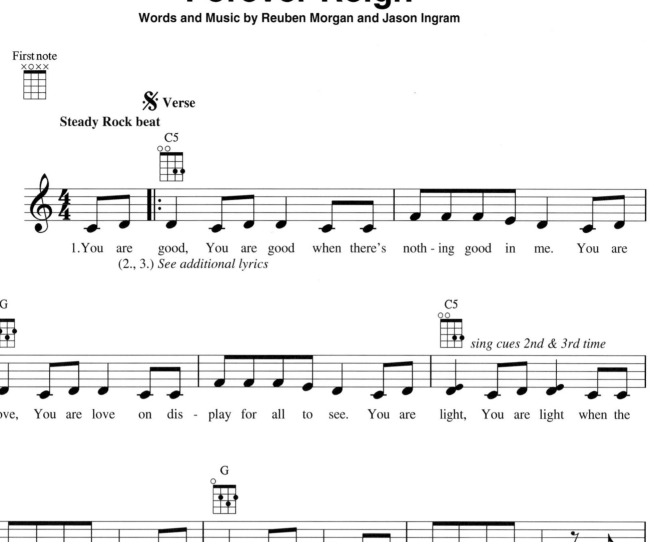

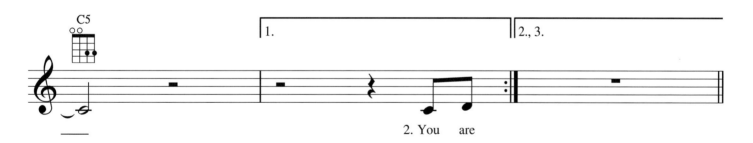

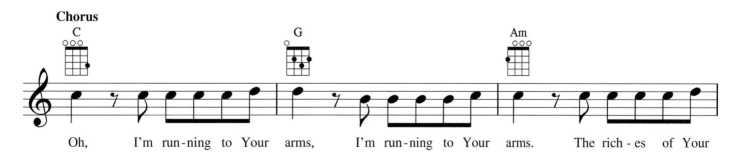

Additional Lyrics

2. You are peace, You are peace when my fear is crippling.
   You are truth, You are truth, even in my wandering.
   You are joy, You are joy; You're the reason that I sing.
   You are life, You are life; in You death has lost its sting, yeah.

3. You are more, You are more than my words will ever say.
   "You are Lord, You are Lord," all creation will proclaim.
   You are here, You are here; in Your presence I'm made whole.
   You are God, You are God; of all else I'm letting go.

Cornerstone

Words and Music by Jonas Myrin, Reuben Morgan, Eric Liljero and Edward Mote

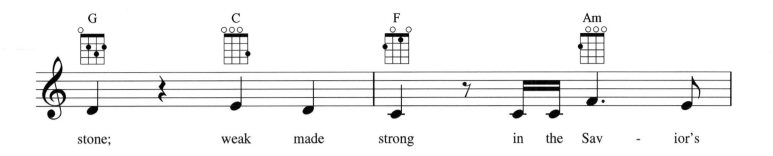

stone;   weak   made   strong   in   the   Sav - ior's

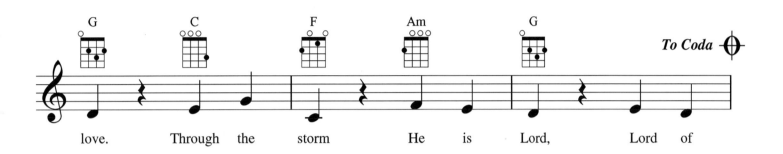

To Coda ⊕

love.   Through   the   storm   He   is   Lord,   Lord   of

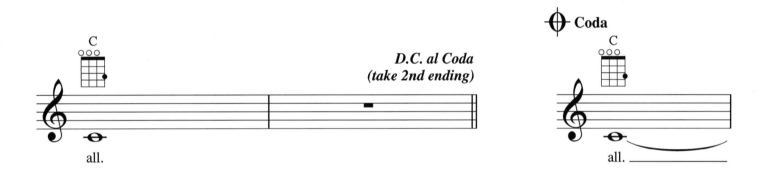

D.C. al Coda
(take 2nd ending)

⊕ **Coda**

all.   all. _____

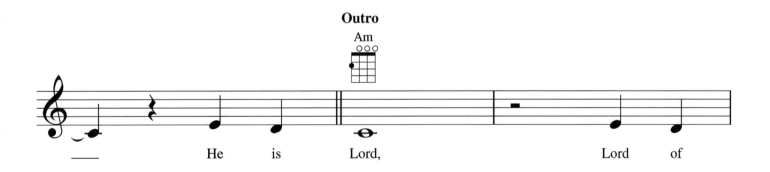

Outro

He   is   Lord,   Lord   of

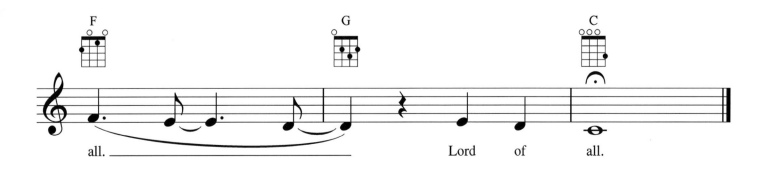

all. _____   Lord   of   all.

Everlasting God

Words and Music by Brenton Brown and Ken Riley

Forever

Words and Music by Chris Tomlin

First note

Verse
Moderately fast

1. Give thanks to the Lord, __ our God and ___ King. __ His
2. With a might - y hand and out - stretched _ arm, __ His
3. From the ris - ing to the set - ting ___ sun, __ His

love en - dures ___ for - ev - er.
love en - dures ___ for - ev - er.
love en - dures ___ for - ev - er. And by the

For He is good, __ He is a - bove all ___ things. __ His
For the life ___ that's been re - born, __ His
grace of ___ God ___ we will car - ry ___ on. __ His

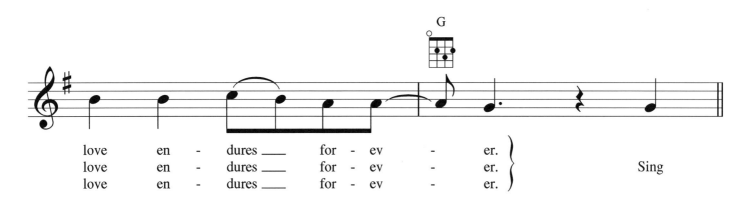

love en - dures ___ for - ev - er.
love en - dures ___ for - ev - er.
love en - dures ___ for - ev - er.

Sing

From the Inside Out

Words and Music by Joel Houston

(Instrumental)

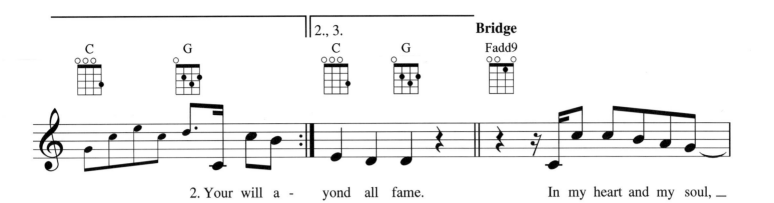

2. Your will a - yond all fame. In my heart and my soul, __

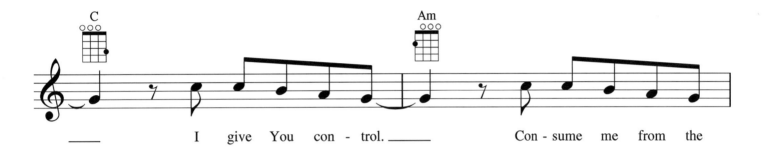

__ I give You con - trol. _____ Con - sume me from the

in - side out, Lord. And let jus - tice and praise __ be - come my em - brace, __

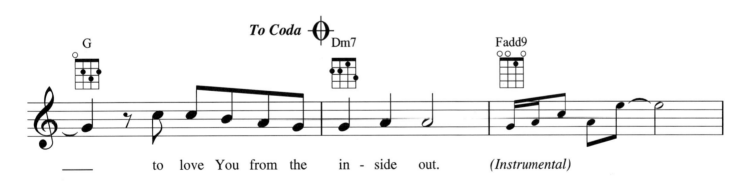

To Coda ⊕

__ to love You from the in - side out. *(Instrumental)*

D.S. al Coda
(take 2nd ending)

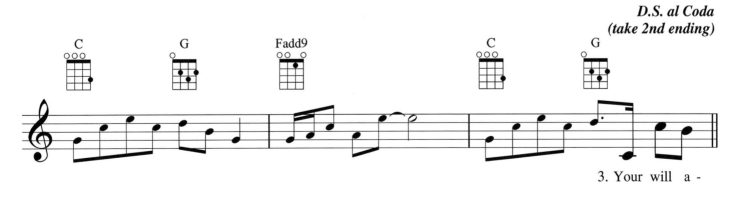

3. Your will a -

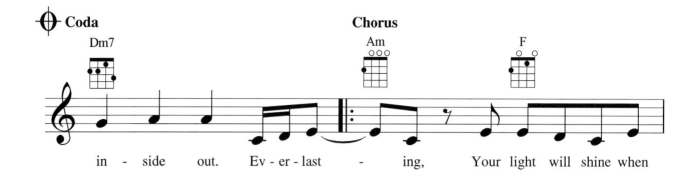

Coda   **Chorus**

in - side out.   Ev - er - last - ing,   Your light will shine when

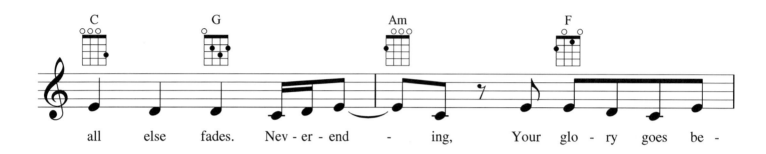

all   else fades.   Nev - er - end - ing,   Your glo - ry goes be -

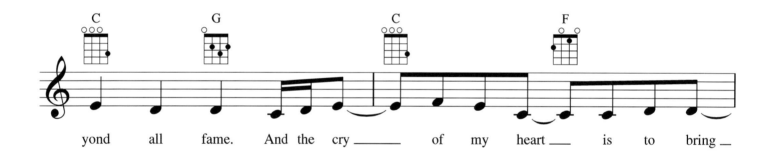

yond   all fame.   And the cry _____ of my heart ___ is to bring _

_____ You praise. From the in - side out, Lord, my soul _

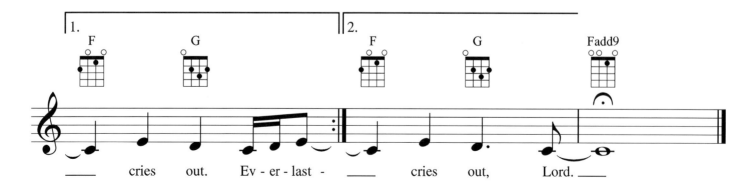

_____ cries out. Ev - er - last -   ___ cries out,   Lord. ____

Great I Am

Words and Music by Jared Anderson

First note

Verse
Moderate Pop beat

1. I wan - na be ____ close, ____ close to Your side, ____
2. I wan - na be ____ near, ____ near to Your heart, _

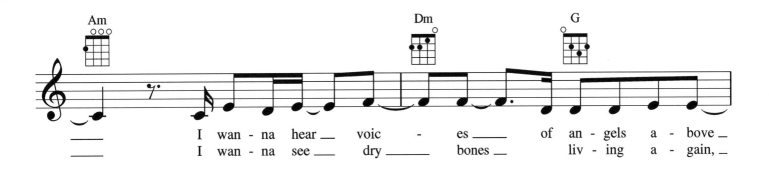

____ so heav - en is ____ real ____ and death is a lie. ____
____ lov - ing the ____ world ____ and hat - ing the dark. ____

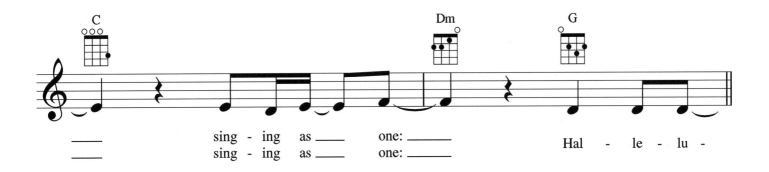

____ I wan - na hear ____ voic - es ____ of an - gels a - bove ____
____ I wan - na see ____ dry ____ bones ____ liv - ing a - gain, _

____ sing - ing as ____ one: ____
____ sing - ing as ____ one: ____

Hal - le - lu -

God Is Able

Words and Music by Reuben Morgan and Ben Fielding

How Deep the Father's Love for Us

Words and Music by Stuart Townend

1. How deep the Fa-ther's love for us, how vast be-yond all meas - ure, that
(2.) hold the Man up - on a cross, my sin up - on His shoul - ders. A-
(3.) will not boast in an - y-thing; no gifts, no pow'r, no wis - dom. But

He should give His on - ly Son to make a wretch His treas - ure. How
shamed, I hear my mock-ing voice call out a - mong the scof - fers. It
I will boast in Je - sus Christ, His death and res - ur - rec - tion. Why

great the pain of sear - ing loss; the Fa - ther turns His face a - way as
was my sin that held Him there un - til it was ac - com - plished. His
should I gain from His re - ward? I can - not give an an - swer. But

wounds which mar the Cho - sen One bring man - y sons to glo -
dy - ing breath has brought me life; I know that it is fin -
this I know with all my heart: His wounds have paid my ran -

ry. 2. Be - som.
ished. 3. I

The Heart of Worship

Words and Music by Matt Redman

through the way things ap - pear; You're look - ing in - to my heart. ___

Chorus

___ I'm com - ing back to the heart ___ of wor - ship, and it's

all a - bout ___ You, ___ all a - bout ___ You, ___ Je - sus.

I'm sor - ry, Lord, for the thing ___ I've made ___ it, when it's

all a - bout ___ You, ___ all a - bout ___ You, ___ Je - sus. ___

___ ___

Hosanna

Words and Music by Brooke Fraser

1. I see the King of Glo - - ry   com - ing on the clouds with fire. __
2. I see a gen - er - a - - tion   ris - ing up to take their place __

__ The whole earth   shakes, __   the whole earth   shakes. __
__ with self - less   faith, __   with self - less   faith. __

I see His love   and mer - - cy ____   wash - ing o - ver   all   our   sin. __
I see a near   re - viv - - al ____   stir - ring as we   pray   and   seek. __

__ The peo - ple   sing, __   the peo - ple   sing. __ }
__ We're on   our   knees, __   we're on   our   knees. __ }   Ho - san -

Chorus

- na, __ ho-san - na, __ ho - san-na in the high - est. ____   Ho - san -

How He Loves

Words and Music by John Mark McMillan

First note

He is ___ jeal - ous for me. ___

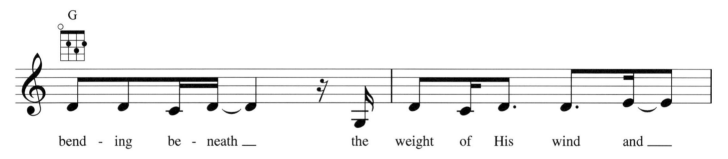

Loves like a hur - ri - cane; I am a tree, ___

bend - ing be - neath ___ the weight of His wind and ___

mer - cy. ___ When all of ___ a sud - den,

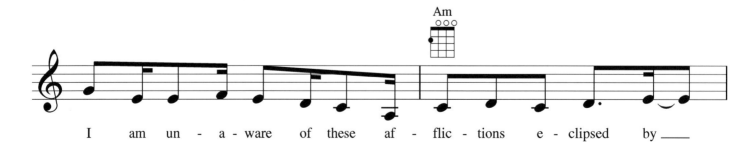

I am un - a - ware of these af - flic - tions e - clipsed by ___

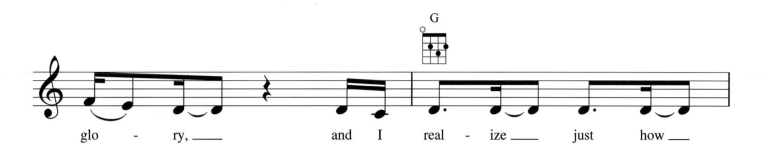

glo - ry, _____ and I real - ize _____ just how _____

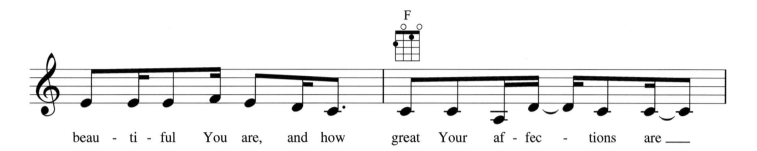

beau - ti - ful You are, and how great Your af - fec - tions are _____

Chorus 1

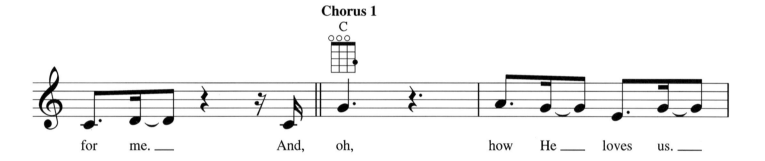

for me. _____ And, oh, how He _____ loves us. _____

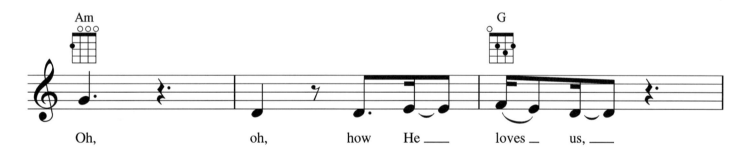

Oh, oh, how He _____ loves _____ us, _____

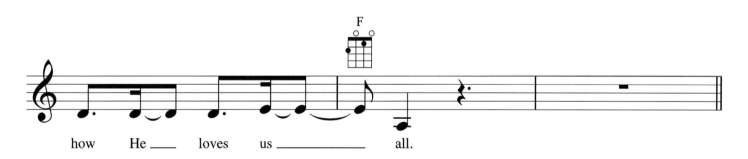

how He _____ loves us _____ all.

Interlude

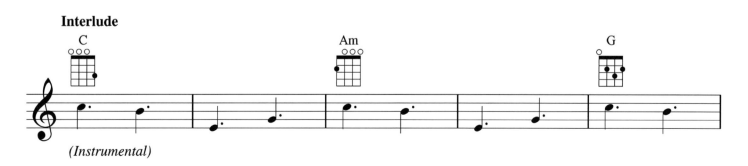

(Instrumental)

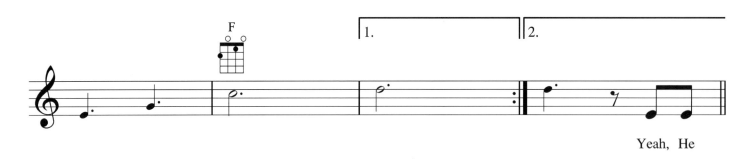

Yeah, He

Chorus 2

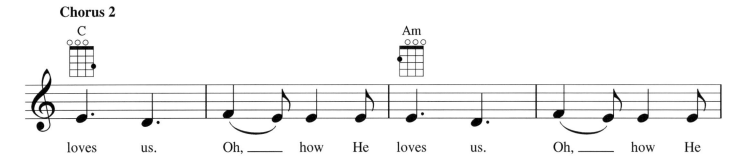

loves   us.   Oh, _____ how   He   loves   us.   Oh, _____ how   He

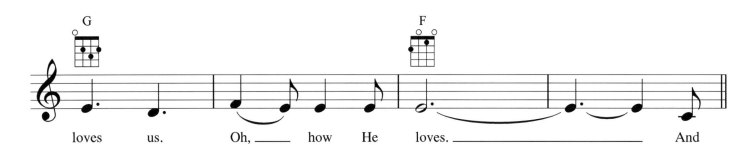

loves   us.   Oh, _____ how   He   loves. _____ And

Bridge

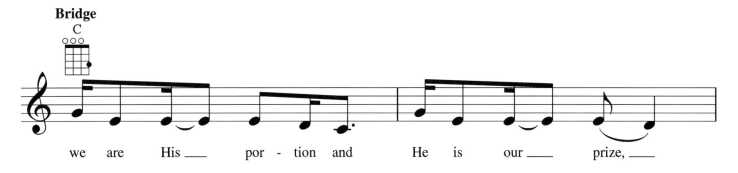

we   are   His __   por - tion   and   He   is   our __   prize, __

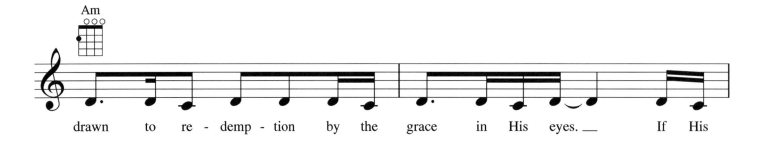

drawn   to   re - demp - tion   by   the   grace   in   His   eyes. __   If   His

grace   is   an __   o - cean, __   we're   all __   sink -   ing. __

And heav-en meets ___ earth like an un-fore-seen kiss, and my

heart turns ___ vio-lent-ly in-side of my chest. I don't have ___ time to main-

tain these re-grets ___ when I think a-bout the way ___

Outro-Chorus

___ that He loves us. Oh, ___ how He loves us.

Oh, ___ how He loves us. Oh, ___ how He loves. ___

Yeah, He loves ___ us ___ all.

I Give You My Heart

Words and Music by Reuben Morgan

Jesus Messiah

Words and Music by Chris Tomlin, Jesse Reeves, Daniel Carson and Ed Cash

1. He be-came __ sin __ who knew no __ sin, __ that
(2.) *See additional lyrics*

we might be-come __ His __ right-eous-ness. He

hum-bled Him-self __ and car-ried the __ cross. __

Love so a-maz-ing, __ love so a-

maz-ing. __ Je-sus Mes-si-ah, __

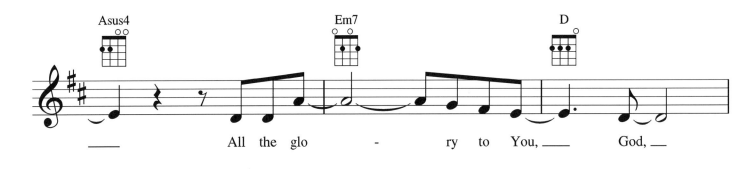

All the glo - - ry to You, ___ God, ___

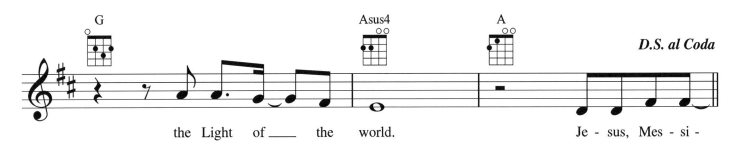

D.S. al Coda

the Light of ___ the world.

Je - sus, Mes - si -

Outro

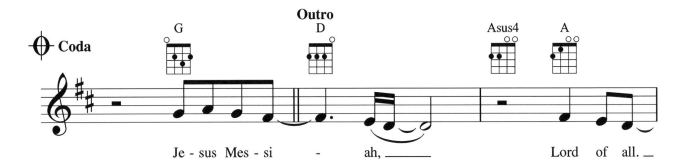

$\oplus$ **Coda**

Je - sus Mes - si - ah, _____

Lord of all. _

___ You're the Lord ___ of all, _____

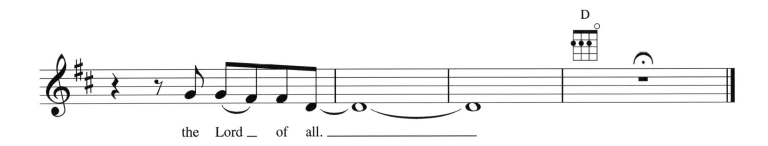

the Lord _ of all. _____

Additional Lyrics

2. His body the bread, His blood the wine,
Broken and poured out, all for love.
The whole earth trembled and the veil was torn.
Love so amazing, love so amazing.

One Thing Remains

(Your Love Never Fails)

Words and Music by Jeremy Riddle, Brian Johnson and Christa Black

Bridge

death, in life, I'm con - fi - dent and cov-ered by ___ the pow'r of Your great

love. My debt is paid; there's noth - ing that can sep - a - rate ___ my

Chorus

heart from Your great love. Your love ___ nev-er fails, it nev-er gives up, it

nev - er runs out on me. Your love ___ nev - er fails, it nev - er gives up, it

nev - er runs out on me. Your love ___ nev - er fails, it nev - er gives up, it

nev-er runs out on me, Your love.

Offering

Words and Music by Paul Baloche

on - ly through __ Your mer - cy, Lord, I come. _____

I bring an of - fer - ing __ of wor - ship to __ my King. _

__ No one on earth __ de - serves __ the prais -

- es that __ I sing. _____ Je - sus, may You __

_____ re - ceive __ the hon - or that __ You're due. _____

O Lord, __ I bring __ an of - fer - ing __ to You. _____

Our God

Words and Music by Jonas Myrin, Chris Tomlin, Matt Redman and Jesse Reeves

- y oth - er. Our God is Heal - er,

awe-some in pow - er, our __ God, __ our __ God. __

__ And if our God is for us,

then who could ev - er stop us? And if our God is with us,

then what could stand a - gainst? __ And if our God is for us,

then who could ev - er stop us? And if our God is with us,

then what could stand a - gainst? __

Overcome

Words and Music by Jon Egan

1. Seat-ed a-bove, en-throned in the Fa-ther's love.

Des-tined to die, poured out for all man-kind.

2. God's on-ly Son, per-fect and spot-less
3. Pow-er in hand, speak-ing the Fa-ther's

One.
plan.

He nev-er sinned, but
Send-ing us out, a

suf-fered as if He did.
light in this bro-ken land.

All au-

Revelation Song

Words and Music by Jennie Lee Riddle

who was and is and is to come.

With all cre - a - tion I sing praise to the King of kings.

You are my ev - 'ry - thing, and I will a - dore You.

To Coda

Verse

2. Clothed in rain - bows of liv - ing col - or,

flash - es of light - ning, rolls of thun - der.

Bless - ing and hon - or, strength _ and glo - ry and pow - er be ____

D.S. al Coda

to You, ____ the on - ly wise King.

Coda

Verse

3. Filled with won - der, awe - struck won - der,

at the men - tion of ____ Your name. ____

Je - sus, Your name _ is pow - er, breath _ and liv - ing wa - ter,

such _ a mar - v'lous mys - ter - y. ____

Chorus

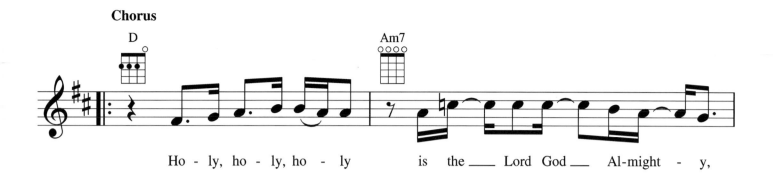

Ho - ly, ho - ly, ho - ly is the ___ Lord God ___ Al-might - y,

who was ___ and is ___ and is ___ to come. ___

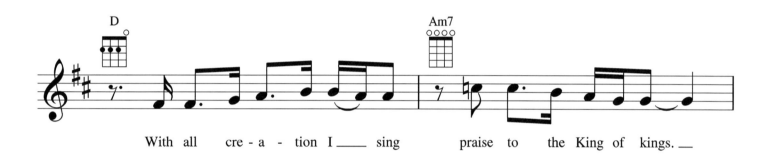

With all cre - a - tion I ___ sing praise to the King of kings. ___

You are my ev - 'ry - thing, ___ and I will ___ a - dore You.

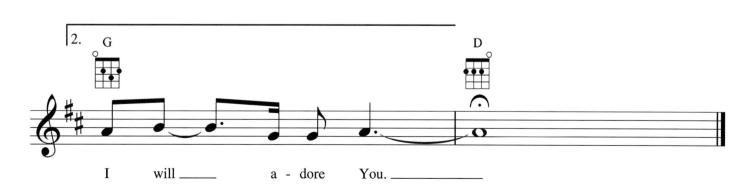

I will ___ a - dore You. ___

The Stand

Words and Music by Joel Houston

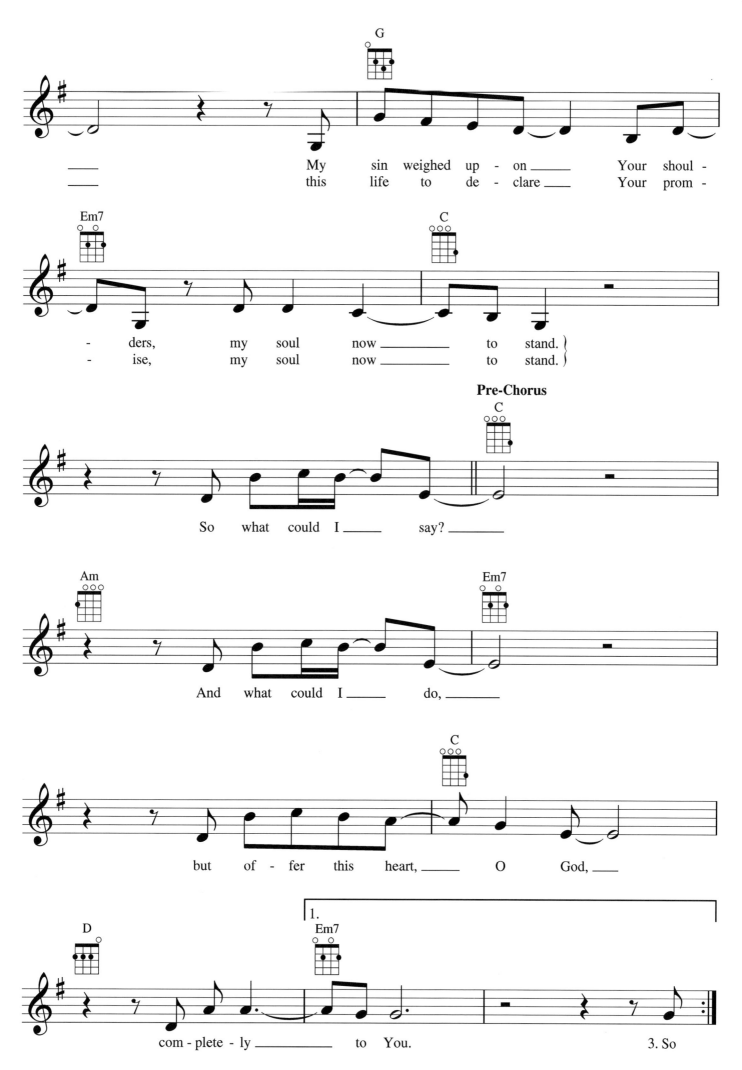

My sin weighed up - on _____ Your shoul -
this life to de - clare _____ Your prom -

- ders, my soul now _____ to stand. }
- ise, my soul now _____ to stand. }

Pre-Chorus

So what could I _____ say? _____

And what could I _____ do, _____

but of - fer this heart, _____ O God, ___

1.

com - plete - ly _____ to You.   3. So

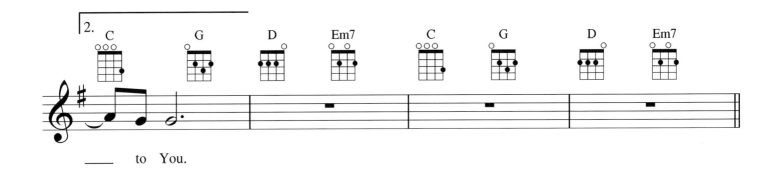

____ to You.

Chorus

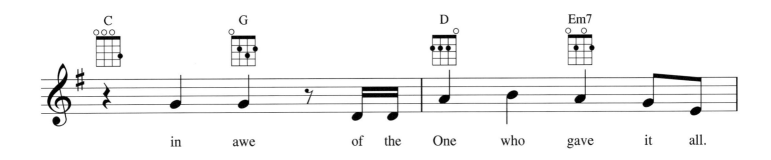

I'll stand with arms high and heart a - ban - doned,

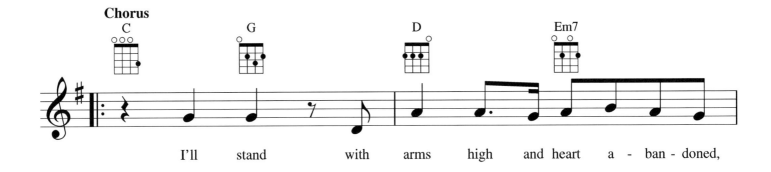

in awe of the One who gave it all.

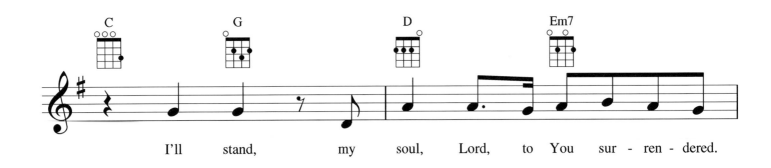

I'll stand, my soul, Lord, to You sur - ren - dered.

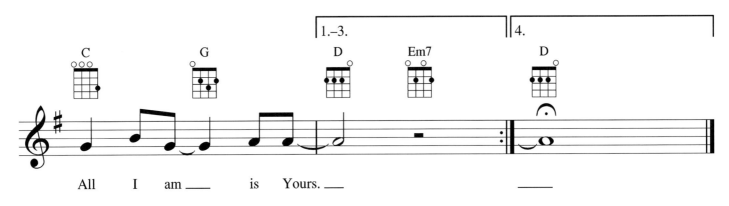

All I am ____ is Yours. ____

Stronger

Words and Music by Ben Fielding and Reuben Morgan

10,000 Reasons
(Bless the Lord)

Words and Music by Jonas Myrin and Matt Redman

Chorus
Moderate Ballad

Bless the Lord, O my soul, O _____ my soul.

Wor-ship His ho - ly name. ___ Sing like nev - er be - fore,

O my soul. I'll wor-ship Your ho - ly name. ___

Verse

1. The sun comes up, it's a new day dawn - ing.
2. You're rich in love and You're slow to an - ger.

It's time to sing Your song _____ a - gain. ___ What -
Your name is great and Your heart is kind. ___ For

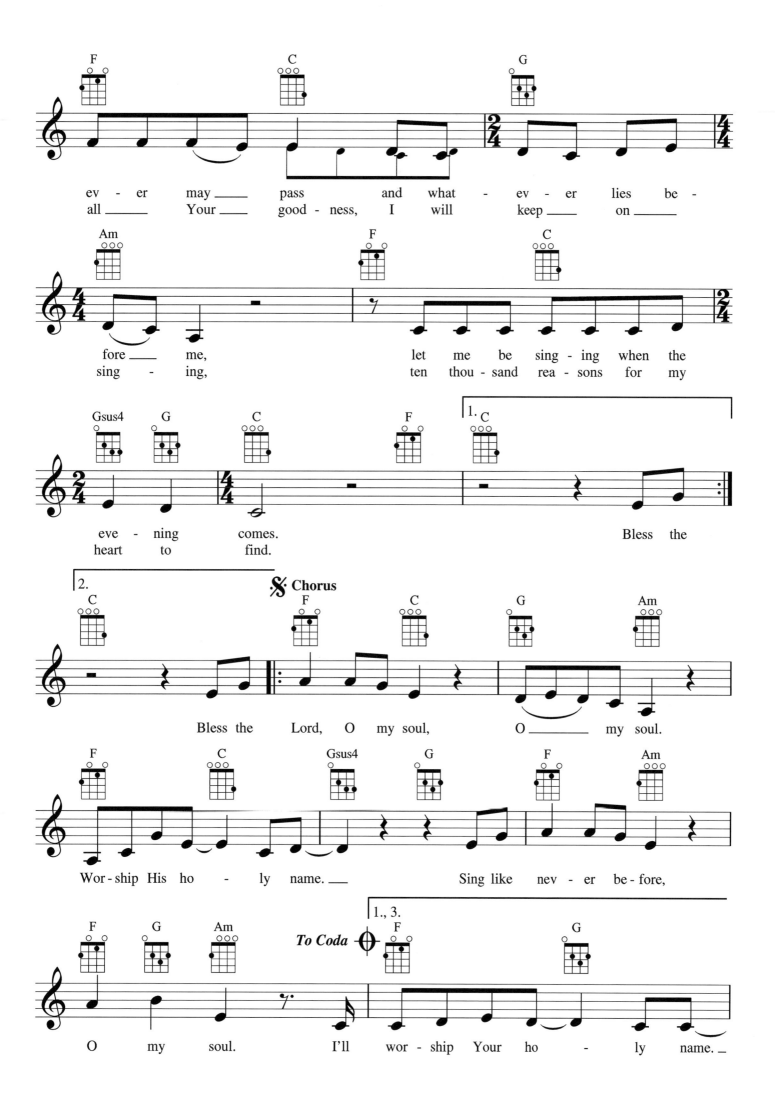

wor - ship Your ho - ly name.

God, I'll wor - ship Your ho - ly name.

Outro

Sing like nev - er be - fore, O my soul. I'll

wor - ship Your ho - ly name. I'll wor - ship Your ho - ly name.

God, I'll wor - ship Your ho - ly name.

Whom Shall I Fear
(God of Angel Armies)

Words and Music by Chris Tomlin, Ed Cash and Scott Cash

Verse
Moderately

1. You hear me when I call, You are my morn - ing song.

Though dark - ness fills the night, it can - not hide the light. _____

Whom shall _____ I _____ fear?

Verse

2. You crush the en - e - my un - der - neath my feet.
3. My strength is in Your name, for You a - lone can save.

You are my sword and shield, though trou - bles lin - ger still. _____
You will de - liv - er me; Yours is the vic - to - ry. _____

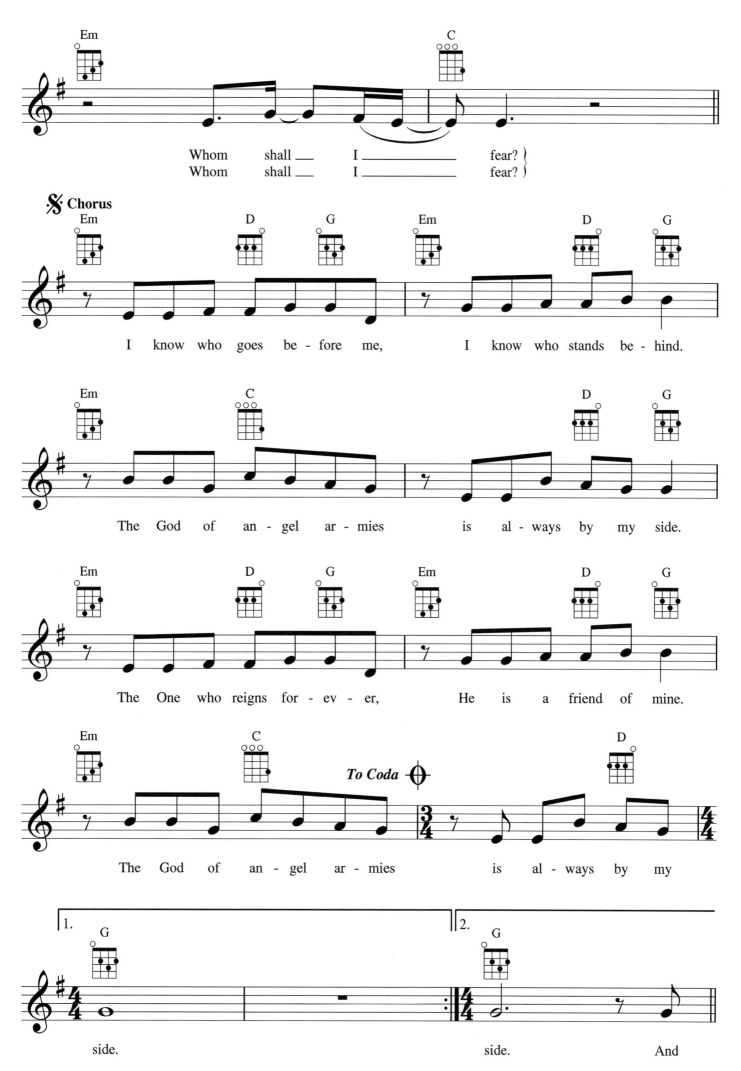

Your Grace Is Enough

Words and Music by Matt Maher

Your Love Never Fails

Words and Music by Anthony Skinner and Chris McClarney

1. Noth - ing ___ can sep - a - rate, e - ven if I
2. *See additional lyrics*

ran a - way. Your ___ love nev - er fails. ___

I know I ___ still make mis - takes, but

You have new mer - cies for me ev - 'ry day. Your ___

___ love nev - er fails. ___

Additional Lyrics

2. The wind is strong and the water's deep,
   But I'm not alone here in these open seas.
   Your love never fails.
   The chasm is far too wide;
   I never thought I'd reach the other side.
   Your love never fails.